The Unofficial

Harry Potter

Party

Book

The Unofficial
Harry Potter
Party
Book

From Monster Books to Potions Class!
Crafts, Games, and Treats

Jessica Fox

ISBN-13: 978-1461037873
ISBN-10: 1461037875
BISAC: Juvenile Nonfiction / Crafts & Hobbies

Contents

Chapter II: Games 75

Chapter III: Treats 97

Index 117

Introduction

The magical world of J.K. Rowling's *Harry Potter* has delighted adults and children alike for the past decade. We've anticipated the release of each print installment and flocked to theaters again and again for the movies. We've come to think of Harry, Ron, and Hermione as friends; we've mourned the deaths of beloved characters like Professor Dumbledore and Dobby; and we've cheered on the Order of the Phoenix as they defended the Wizarding world against the Dark Lord and his Death Eaters. Now it's time to bring this fantastical world home.

The Unofficial Harry Potter Party Book has been created to help you throw the most magical of Harry Potter parties. With a variety of low-cost, simple-to-prepare crafts, games, and treats, you and your guests will have a blast revisiting the very best of Hogwarts. Most of the activities are suitable for either children or adults; simply modify games as needed to make them as age-appropriate as you wish.

What better way is there to kick off a Harry Potter party than with an Owl-Post Invitation? And, how else does one get to Hogwarts except through Platform 9 ¾? As you look through each of these sections, let your imagination run wild. Use the crafts as decorations, party favors, or prizes.

Just remember, since "the wand chooses the wizard," you may want to have your Wands made up ahead of time, ready for guests to pick up at Ollivander's as they begin their adventure.

The Sorting Hat Ceremony will be a huge hit, too. Where else besides Hogwarts will students see a hat that actually talks?

Get creative with the Potions from Chapter III. There's no need to have everything prepared beforehand. Make a couple of these in "class" and watch your guests delight as their cauldrons bubble over.

If you are thinking of trying the Tri-Wizard Tournament, how about filling the trophy cup with a batch of Dragon Eggs to celebrate victory?

Award your "students" with House Points after each game so they can earn a trip to Hogsmeade. Make sure they each have a pocketful of Galleons to splurge on treats from Honeydukes while they're there! Perhaps younger guests would enjoy making their very own Pygmy Puff to take back to Hogwarts with them.

If the party is for children, convince the adults to get in the spirit by donning robes and helping out as Hogwarts teachers. If the crowd is older, mix in some trivia to keep things interesting. As you plan your event, remember to allow extra time for the magic to take over.

Games may get silly, but that's all part of the fun!

The Unofficial

Harry Potter

Party

Book

CHAPTER I

CRAFTS

$\mathscr{A}$re you ready to make magic? This chapter is filled with easy-to-make crafts that will magically turn your home into Hogwarts. Your party guests enter the magical realm through Platform 9 ¾, marked by your official sign, and proceed to the Great Hall where they'll be sorted into houses by the wise Sorting Hat.

For a great party starter, have your guests make No-Sew Ties according to whichever house they belong to. Or, have their ties made up ahead of time and get straight to the games. Hogwarts students love casting their first spells, and your guests will, too, with their one-of-a-kind Wands. Then they can create their own Remembrall so they won't ever forget how much fun they had at Hogwarts.

Whether you make these crafts ahead of time or have guests make one or two of their own, your party guests will be amazed with all the crafty creations and delightful decorations surrounding them as they immerse themselves into the world of witchcraft and wizardry.

Crystal Ball

DIFFICULTY: 2/5

COST: $1-$3

TIME: 20 MIN.

SUPPLIES

- ❖ 1 Clear Glass Ornament
- ❖ 1 Extra Small Flower Pot Saucer
- ❖ Gold Paint
- ❖ Hot Glue Gun
- ❖ Hot Glue Sticks
- ❖ Pearl Stickers (optional)
- ❖ Mini Water Diamonds (optional)
- ❖ 1 Cotton Ball (optional)

In *Harry Potter and the Deathly Hallows*,
Professor Trelawney hurls her crystal balls at Death
Eaters in an effort to help save Hogwarts.

I.   Remove the metal top from the glass ornament.
     Optional: Fill the ornament with mini water diamonds (clear gel crystals available at craft stores), then seal it off by pushing a cotton ball into the base of the ornament.

II. Turn the flower pot saucer upside down. Paint it gold. Let it dry for about an hour. This will be the base of your crystal ball.

III. Add accents to the base like pearl stickers, glitter, or beads once it's dry.

IV. Squirt hot glue around the top opening of the ornament. Turn the ornament upside down and glue it to the center of the flower pot saucer.

V.   Add accents around the base to hide any excess glue.

That's all there is to it. Use this as a centerpiece, a decoration, or as a prop in divination class.

Extendable Ears

Difficulty: 2/5

Cost: $2-$3

Time: 20 min.

SUPPLIES

- ❖ 2 oz. Package of Flesh-Colored Sculpey or Modeling Clay
- ❖ 2 ft. of Kitchen Twine
- ❖ Pencil

I.   To shape the ears, start by making a thick heart shape out of the Sculpey. Cut it in half down the center of the heart. You now have the beginnings of two ears.

II. Use the eraser of a pencil to press into the ears to create the details.

III. Be sure to make a large hole in the ears where you would find one in a real ear.

IV. Bake the Sculpey or modeling clay according to the time indicated on the packaging.

V.   Once the ears have cooled, tie knots through the holes with the ends of the kitchen twine.

These ears make great decorations, but sadly, they're completely useless for spying.

14:38:15 13-Jul-2023
Ada Public Library
107 E 4th Ave
Ada, MN 56510
218-784-4480

Reference#: 204906

1. The unofficial Harry Potter
party book : from monster
books to potions class! : crafts,
games and treats
Barcode: 33500010889947
Due Date: 08-03-2023

2. Questionable creatures : a
bestiary
Barcode: 33500093906715
Due Date: 08-03-2023

No-Sew House Tie

DIFFICULTY: 3/5

COST: $1-$3

TIME: 15 MIN.

SUPPLIES

- ❖ 1 Piece of Red Felt
- ❖ 1 Piece of Gold Felt
- ❖ Scissors
- ❖ Hot Glue Gun
- ❖ Hot Glue Sticks
- ❖ Bar Pins

I. Draw the shape of a tie on the back of a piece of red felt. Cut out the tie.

II. Cut out several thin strips of gold felt about half an inch tall and 3 inches wide. Arrange them horizontally on the felt tie and hot glue them to the tie. Cut off all the excess felt.

III. Sew or hot glue a bar pin to the top back part of the tie.

Get several different colors of felt to create house ties for each house.

House Colors:

Gryffindor: Red and Gold

Hufflepuff: Yellow and Black

Ravenclaw: Blue and Bronze
(Blue and Grey in films)

Slytherin: Green and Silver

Galleons

DIFFICULTY: 1/5

TIME: 10 MIN.

COST: $8-$10

SUPPLIES

❖ Gold Sculpey or Modeling Clay
❖ Miniature Alphabet Stamps

DIRECTIONS

I. Flatten out the gold Sculpey with a rolling pin. Use a small round cookie cutter or upside down bud vase to cut circles out of the Sculpey.

II. Use alphabet stamps to stamp the word "GALLEON" into the Sculpey.

III. Press your thumbnail into the Sculpey around the edges of the coins to give them ridges.

IV. Bake the coins according to the time indicated on the Sculpey packaging.

V. Use other colors to create knuts and sickles.

IMPORTANT:

Don't get caught or the Ministry of Magic will put you
in Azkaban for counterfeiting!

Platform Sign

DIFFICULTY: 3/5

COST: $2-$3

TIME: 10 MIN.

SUPPLIES

- ❖ 1 Red Poster Board
- ❖ Black Alphabet Stickers
- ❖ Circle Punch
- ❖ 1 Sheet of White Paper
- ❖ Glue

I.   Cut the red poster board in half.

II.   Use the circle punch to cut out two circles in the top corners of the sign.

III.   Use the black alphabet stickers to spell out "Hogwarts Express" on the bottom of the sign.

IV.   Using your computer, print out "9 3/4" on a white piece of paper.

V.   Place a bowl over the center of the numbers and trace around it with a pencil to make a perfect circle.

VI.   Cut out the circle and glue it to the center of the sign.

Hang the sign above your door or below your mailbox before the party and there will be no doubt where to go to enter Hogwarts.

House Points

DIFFICULTY: 1/5

TIME: 5 MIN.

COST: $8-$10

SUPPLIES

- ❖ 4 Bud Vases
- ❖ 1 bag of Red Vase Gems
- ❖ 1 bag of Blue Vase Gems
- ❖ 1 bag of Green Vase Gems
- ❖ 1 bag of Yellow Vase Gems

Fill each bud vase with a few gems for each house as guests arrive.

Red: Gryffindor
Blue: Ravenclaw
Green: Slytherin
Yellow: Hufflepuff

Use the house points to reward the guests by giving gems to their houses throughout the party whenever someone from that house wins a game or answers a question correctly.

The house with the most gems at the end of the party is the House Cup winner.

Mandrake

DIFFICULTY: 2/5

COST: $3-$6

TIME: 10 MIN.

SUPPLIES

- ❖ Artificial Leaves
- ❖ 1 Celery Root
- ❖ Brown Paint
- ❖ Black Paint
- ❖ Pink Paint
- ❖ 1 Fine-Tip Paintbrush
- ❖ 1 Flower Pot
- ❖ 1 Cup of Soil

I.   Paint a face on your celery root - as cute or as menacing as you like.

II.   Push the leaves into the top of the celery root. This is easy to do because the celery root is firm, but soft inside.

III.   Put some soil into the pot and put your mandrake into the soil.

Tip: You can find celery root in your local grocery store near the ginger.

Make sure to put on some earmuffs before you take your new mandrake out of its pot!

Neville Longbottom is a star Herbology student. What plant does he carry with him to Hogwarts at the beginning of fifth year?

Answer: Mimbulus Mimbletonia

Owl Post Invitation

DIFFICULTY: 4/5

COST: $1-$2

TIME: 5-10 MIN.

SUPPLIES

- ❖ 1 Black Permanent Marker
- ❖ 1 Yellow Permanent Marker
- ❖ 1 White Helium-Filled Balloon
- ❖ 2 ft. of Kitchen Twine
- ❖ 1 Invitation

I. Starting with a helium-filled balloon, draw yellow eyes at the top of the balloon. Line the yellow eyes with black marker and add big, black pupils.

II. Add the beak, feet, details of the feathers, and spots.

III. When the marker has dried, tie a long piece of kitchen twine to the bottom of the balloon.

IV. Tie the invitation near the bottom of the balloon using the twine.

V. Put a weight on the end of the twine.

Leave the Owl Post invitation on your invitee's doorstep, ring the doorbell and make a run for it!

You may know that Harry picked the name Hedwig for his new Snowy Owl from a book on magic, but did you know that the 3 owls that play Hedwig in the films are named Gizmo, Ook, and Sprout?

Potion Bottles

DIFFICULTY: 2/5

COST: $1-$8

TIME: 15 MIN.

SUPPLIES

- ❖ Assorted Glass Jars
- ❖ 1 Sheet of Paper
- ❖ Brown Paint
- ❖ 1 Cup of Water
- ❖ 1 Black Marker
- ❖ Coffee Filters
- ❖ Kitchen Twine
- ❖ Glue
- ❖ Decorative Edge Scissors

I.   Mix the tube of brown paint with the water.

II.   Dip the coffee filters and paper into the brown paint/water mixture. Let them dry.

III.   Cut labels out of the paper with the decorative edge scissors.

IV.   If you'd like darker paper, dip your paper in the brown paint again.

V.   Go around the edges of the labels with a black marker.

VI.   Write the name of your ingredient on the label.

VII.   Put a coffee filter over the top of the jar and tie it securely with the kitchen twine.

Go give Snape a run for his galleons.

Tip: For tall, slim bottles, use cupcake baking cups instead of coffee filters.

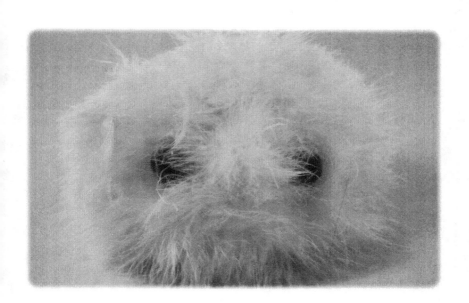

Pygmy Puff

DIFFICULTY: 2/5

COST: $1-$4

TIME: 5 MIN.

SUPPLIES

- ❖ 1 Foam Ball
- ❖ 1 Pink or Purple Feather Boa
- ❖ 2 Glass Beads or Buttons
- ❖ Hot Glue Gun
- ❖ Hot Glue Sticks

I.   Add hot glue to the foam ball while slowly wrapping the feather boa around it. Completely cover the ball with the boa, and check for any bald spots.

II.   When the glue has cooled, add glass beads or buttons to the center of the ball for eyes.

Tip: Young children can use Elmer's glue for this project – it will just take a little longer to dry.

Cheap, easy, and adorable. These pygmy puffs make great party favors.

> Ginny has a beloved purple Pygmy Puff named Arnold. Encourage your guests to name their pygmy puffs, too!

No-Mess Quills

DIFFICULTY: 1/5

COST: $1-$3

TIME: 3-5 MIN.

SUPPLIES

- ❖ 1 Large Feather
- ❖ 1 Push-Up Pencil
- ❖ 1 Pen with Removable Parts
- ❖ Super Glue
- ❖ Scissors

DIRECTIONS

These quills are easy to make and allow everyone at your party to use a quill without spilling black ink all over your floor. After all, Hermione won't be around to clean up all those ink spills.

I.   Cut the tip off the end of the feather.

II.   If you want a feather *pencil*, remove the leaded caps from the push-up pencil. Put a small amount of super glue inside the leaded cap. Push the leaded cap onto the end of the feather. Let it dry.

III. If you want a feather *pen*, remove the ink tube from inside the pen. Squirt a small amount of super glue into the hollow part of the end of the feather and then push the ink tube into the feather. Let it dry.

Hermione uses the spell "Tergeo" to clean spilled ink off Ron's Defense Against the Dark Arts essay.

Luna's

Radish Earrings

DIFFICULTY: 3/5

COST: $3-$5

TIME: 20 MIN.

SUPPLIES

- ❖ ½ oz. White Sculpey or Modeling Clay
- ❖ ½ oz. Red Sculpey or Modeling Clay
- ❖ 2 Small Artificial Leaves
- ❖ 2 Eye Pins
- ❖ 2 Earrings

Luna is well-known for her radish earrings,
but what piece of jewelry does she
wear to keep the Nargles away?

Answer: A Butterbeer Cork Necklace

DIRECTIONS

I.   Roll out two balls of red Sculpey.

II.   Roll out two ball of white Sculpey.

III.   Push the red balls of Sculpey into the white balls of Sculpey and roll it together until you have two balls that are half red and half white.

IV.   Pull and twist the bottoms of the white Sculpey until it resembles a radish.

V.   Make a hole in the top, red part of the radish.

VI.   Push the small artificial leaves into the radish.

VII.   Behind the leaves, insert the eye pins. Then hook the earrings into the eye pins.

VIII. Bake the radish earrings according to the time indicated on the Sculpey packaging.

When you wear these earrings, you'll look simply radishing!

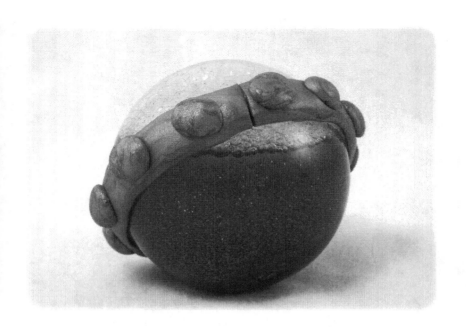

Remembrall

DIFFICULTY: 3/5

COST: $2-$4

TIME: 20 MIN.

SUPPLIES

- ❖ Gold Sculpey or Modeling Clay
- ❖ Glitter-Filled Ball
- ❖ Knife
- ❖ Hot Glue Gun
- ❖ Hot Glue Sticks

DIRECTIONS

I. Roll out the gold Sculpey into a long rope. Wrap the rope around the center of the ball and then flatten it onto the ball.

II. For smoother edges, use the knife to cut the sides of the Sculpey so that it's even.

III. Roll small balls out of gold Sculpey and flatten them around the band you've created around the ball.

IV. Carefully cut the band into two pieces on opposite sides of the ball and remove them from the surface of the ball. Make sure to retain the curved shape.

V. Bake the Sculpey for the time indicated on the packaging.

VI. After it cools, glue the pieces back onto the center of the ball.

Remembralls make great gifts or prizes for the party.

Sorting Hat

DIFFICULTY: 3/5

COST: $1 OR LESS

TIME: 15 MIN.

SUPPLIES

- ❖ 1 Brown Paper Grocery Bag
- ❖ 1 Large Piece of Brown Paper
- ❖ Tape
- ❖ Hot Glue Gun
- ❖ Hot Glue Sticks
- ❖ Scissors

DIRECTIONS

I.   Carefully turn the paper grocery bag inside out without tearing it.

II.   Crumple the bag until it has plenty of deep and thin creases.

III.   Cut a long slit from the bottom to the top of the bag. Shape the bag into a cone shape and tape or glue it securely. Trim any excess from the bottom of the cone.

IV.   Sculpt the bag by making very deep creases for the brow and the mouth. Go inside the bag with your hand and tape the creases from the inside to secure them.

V.   Cut a very large circle out of the brown paper to create a brim for the hat.

VI.   Hot glue the sculpted cone to the center of the circle of paper.

VII.   Cut a hole out of the center of the circle of paper.

Check out how to create your own Sorting Ceremony with your new Sorting Hat on page 77.

Magical Tags

DIFFICULTY: 2/5

COST: $1-$5

TIME: 5 MIN.

SUPPLIES

- ❖ Kraft Paper
- ❖ Decorative Edge Scissors

DIRECTIONS

Turn all your ordinary toy prizes into something more magical by removing the original cardboard tag and replacing it with one that reads, "Zonko's Joke Shop" or "Weasley's Wizard Wheezes."

I. Remove the original tags from your toys.

II. Type up your new tag's text on your computer and print it out on kraft paper.

III. Cut the tag out using decorative edge scissors.

IV. Staple the corners of the tag onto the plastic bag where the old tag used to be.

If you want to package up some crafts you've made from this book, just place them inside thin, clear sandwich bags and staple your new tags to the top.

Wands

DIFFICULTY: 3/5

COST: $3-$5

TIME: 30 MIN.

SUPPLIES

- ❖ 12 Inch Wooden Dowel
- ❖ White Sculpey or Modeling Clay
- ❖ Brown Paint
- ❖ Gold Paint
- ❖ Hot Glue Gun
- ❖ Hot Glue Sticks

DIRECTIONS

I.   Use the wooden dowel as the base for the wand. Mash Sculpey over it and sculpt it into the shape you want for your wand.

II.   Bake the wand according to the time indicated on the Sculpey packaging.

III. When it cools, use the hot glue gun to add texture, vines, or handles to the wand.

IV.   Paint the wand brown and add gold accents.

Tip: Rubber cement makes for a good hot glue alternative for small children.

Note: The picture of example wands includes one finished wand without a handle and one un-finished wand with a handle. The un-finished wand illustrates what your wand will look like before adding paint and glue.

This is a fun activity for all ages and makes for a great souvenir.

Expelliarmus!

Monster Book

of

Monsters

DIFFICULTY: 5/5

COST: $10-$15

TIME: 1 – 2 HOURS

SUPPLIES

- ❖ 1 Plain Book Box (Available at Craft Stores)
- ❖ White Sculpey or Modeling Clay
- ❖ Red Sculpey or Modeling Clay
- ❖ Black Sculpey or Modeling Clay
- ❖ White Paint
- ❖ Yellow Paint
- ❖ 2 Feet of Brown Faux Fur
- ❖ 1 Cup of Poly-fil or Cotton Balls
- ❖ Hot Glue Gun
- ❖ Hot Glue Sticks

I.   Paint the sides of the book box white so that it looks like it's filled with pages. Let dry.

II.   Glue poly-fil or cotton balls to the top middle of the box to give the monster a bit of a snout.

III.   Create two large fangs out of the white Sculpey. Bake according to the Sculpey directions. Once cool, glue them to the top opening of the box.

IV.   Hot glue the faux fur over the poly-fil or cotton balls, to the top, spine, and bottom of the book box. Trim the excess fur.

V.   Use the red Sculpey to create the gums of the monster.

VI.   Use the white Sculpey to create the teeth of the monster. Bake the teeth according to the Sculpey directions.

VII.   Once the teeth have cooled, press them into the back of the unbaked Sculpey gums, allowing most of the tooth to protrude.

VIII.   Bake the gums with the teeth still inside them.

IX.   Once cool, paint the teeth with yellow paint to give your monster an even scarier look.

X.   Roll four balls out of the black Sculpey. Press holes into them and squeeze them so they look a bit like pitted olives. Bake. These will be the eyes.

XI.   Hot glue the eyes and gums with teeth to the appropriate places on the fur.

XII.   Give your monster book a jagged haircut so he'll look wilder.

Optional: Wrap a belt around your monster book to keep him from biting your ankles.

CHAPTER II

CLASSES & GAMES

*I*t might be a party, but there is always time to learn. With these games your "students" will learn how to make potions, care for magical creatures, grow magical plants, and defend themselves against the Dark Arts. Who doesn't need to know that?

Between classes, students can relive Harry's adventures in the Tri-Wizard Tournament, fend off werewolves, or take a whack at the Dark Mark Piñata. Perhaps Dobby will show up to help win the House Elf Relay. Don't forget to sharpen those Quidditch skills because you'll be dodging Bludgers, scoring points, and seeking that Snitch to take your team to Quidditch victory!

A variety of games are provided for all ages. Everyone has a chance to win House Points, prizes, and to hone their wizardry skills. Be sure to allow plenty of time for fun and laughs with each of these games.

Keep an eye out for that party-pooper, Professor Snape. He's never much fun.

Sorting Ceremony

This game is a lot of fun, but be careful - some people don't take kindly to being sorted into Slytherin.

To set this game up, you'll need to make or buy a Sorting Hat. Directions for making your own Sorting Hat can be found on page 61.

Before the party, tape a cell phone inside the Sorting Hat and set it to speaker phone mode.

Before guests arrive, call the cell phone from another phone and turn the volume of the cell phone up as high as it will go.

When the sorting ceremony begins, have someone on the other end of the cell phone pretend to be the voice of the Sorting Hat.

Another person should control the hat by carefully placing it over the tops of the guests' heads while concealing the cell phone.

The Sorting Hat will now be able to magically talk and place students into their appropriate houses.

Tip: Practice a few times beforehand and you should have a pretty convincing talking Sorting Hat by the time the party comes around.

Care of Magical Creatures

Perhaps Hagrid's flobberworms would have been more interesting to students if they had been in a flobberworm race.

For this class, you're going to need some red wiggler worms (you can get these at a fishing shop), a large white poster board, and a spray bottle filled with water.

Draw a large circle on the poster board. Draw a small circle in the middle of the poster board by tracing around a can.

Place the red wiggler worms in the middle of the circle. These will be your flobberworms.

Have students name all the flobberworms – this is half the fun. Let each student choose the flobberworm that they think will win.

Now spray the worms with a little water (the worms like this and it causes them to start wiggling).

Have the students cheer on their flobberworms!

The first flobberworm to wiggle outside the edges of the large circle is the champion.

When your worms are tuckered out from racing, you'll need to find a good home for them. These types of worms thrive on decaying organic material, so they'd be happy to retire to a vegetable garden or compost heap. Or you can simply return them to the fishing shop.

Although flobberworms generally don't require much care, the ones in Hagrid's class eventually died after having been fed too much lettuce.

Charms Class

The difference between a charm and other types of spells is that charms add or change qualities of something, but don't completely alter it.

For charms class, buy a variety of washable hair colors and hair glitter in spray cans from your local party store.

Students will be able to cast a Hair Color Changing Charm on other students or on themselves using the washable hair colors and their wands.

For a magical effect, have the student close her eyes while you cast the charm, and spray a stripe of color in her hair while her eyes are closed.

When the student opens her eyes, have your wand pointed right at the stripe in her hair.

When she looks in a mirror, she'll see that you've magically changed her hair color with your charm.

Tip: If you've already divided students into houses in The Sorting Game, use the student's house color for her hair color.

Herbology

For this class, you'll need:

- ❖ Several Small Flower Pots
- ❖ 1 Box of Oreos
- ❖ Walnuts
- ❖ Several Very Small Pumpkins
- ❖ Assorted Small Candies

First, crumble the Oreos up to make a "soil" for the "seeds."

Next, open the walnuts and scrape them out until they're clean inside.

Now cut up small strips of paper that, when folded, will fit inside the cleaned out walnut.

Finally, cut the tops off the small pumpkins like you're going to make a jack o' lantern and scrape them out until they're clean.

When you start the class, instruct students to pick the type of plant they would like to grow. Here are some examples:

Kisskin - Fill the pumpkin with Hershey's Kisses.
Pepperkin - Fill the pumpkin with York Peppermint Patties.
Gummykin - Fill the pumpkin with gummy candies.

Instruct the students to write down the name of the plant they'd like to grow on the strip of paper and put it inside the walnut.

Then have them put the walnut in the flower pot and cover it in Oreo "soil."

Have the students cast a growing spell on their seeds and label their flower pot with their name.

Tell the class that they're dismissed while the spell is working on the seeds, but they may return before they leave Hogwarts to pick up their plants.

When the students are busy with another class or game, take the pots to a more discrete location and read the papers inside the walnuts and then remove the walnuts.

Fill the pumpkin with the student's desired candy, put the lid back on the pumpkin, and place it on top of the Oreo soil.

Put the flower pots back in their original spots and enjoy the look of amazement on your students' faces when they come back to find candy-filled pumpkins in their flower pots

Potions Class

This potions class is going to be a little less "bottled fame" and a little more slimy fun.

You'll need 1 bottle of glue per student, some green food coloring, water, and some borax (it's non-toxic and can be found in the laundry section of your local grocery store).

Pour all the bottles of glue into a large bowl, add a few drops of green food coloring, and label it "Troll Snot".

In another bowl, add 3 cups of water and 3 tablespoons of borax. Label it "Fluffy's Drool".

Instruct your students to add 1 cup of Troll Snot to their cauldron (pick these up at a party or craft store) and a tablespoon of Fluffy's Drool. Instruct them to mix it together and if the consistency is too runny, add a bit more of Fluffy's Drool until it has a stretchy, slimy texture.

When students have finished creating their slime, you can give them extras to add to it like sticky eyeballs and sticky rats.

Give students labeled plastic baggies so they can take their slimy creations home.

Dark Mark

Piñata

If there's one thing that would be fun to beat senseless, wouldn't it be the dark mark?

Unfortunately, you can't just run to the party store and buy a dark mark piñata. But you can easily make one.

Just pick up a skull piñata from your local party store along with three identical rubber snakes while you're there.

Cut the heads off two of the snakes and hot glue all the snakes together so that you have one very long snake.

Cut a hole in the mouth of the skull to wind the rubber snake through, then wrap the snake around itself in the shape of an 8, just like the dark mark. Now it's ready for a beating.

Don't forget to put the candy inside or you'll be next!

Guess the Animagus

If you're looking for a quieter game that can be played anywhere, this is it.

Starting from the youngest, each player thinks of what type of animagus they would most like to be.

Then that player gives hints about what their animagus is, and all the other players try to guess what animal it could be.

For example, if you chose a llama as your animagus, you could start with more difficult clues like, "I'm a mammal" and "I eat grass" and move on to easier clues like, "I will spit right in your eye if you even consider putting those stinky food pellets in my face."

Hot Dragon Eggs

If you have some leftover plastic Easter eggs, a glue gun, and some black and gold paint, you've already got all the supplies you need to make the dragon eggs for this game.

Paint the eggs inside and out with the black paint and let them dry. Use your hot glue gun to glue lines and grooves over the egg to give it some cool texture like you did with the wands in the Crafts chapter. Let the glue harden, then paint over the glue with gold paint.

You can fill the eggs with whatever treats you like – plastic dragon toys, candy rocks, gold coins, money, etc. To make it more exciting, put different items in each different egg, so the player who wins the egg will be totally surprised.

Paint enough eggs so that each of the players can have one.

To play, you'll need a CD of some magical music and a CD player.

Gather all the players into a circle, start the music, and start passing one of the eggs around.

Let the music play for 20-30 seconds, then stop the music.

Whoever is holding the egg when the music stops is out, but they get to keep their new dragon egg, open it up and take out their prize.

Keep playing until you run out of eggs!

House Elf Relay

In this game, all the players must work together as house elves to finish all their chores before the other team does.

This game works best outside so that your little house elves have plenty of room to play in.

For the first leg of the relay, the house elves must find 6 bouncy balls hidden around the yard and throw them into their waste bin. Each team should have their own bin. If a ball bounces out of the bin, they must put it back in.

For the second leg of the relay, the house elf who cleaned up the bouncy balls races them over to the next house elf. This house elf must take out one of the balls, put it on a large wooden spoon, and race it over to the next house elf without letting the ball fall off.

For the third leg of the relay, the next house elf will take the spoon from the previous house elf and dig in a bucket full of dirt or sand for a sock inside a sandwich bag.

The longer and more colorful the sock, the more fun.

They must use the spoon to dig and pull out the bag. No hands! Once they retrieve the bag, they must take their shoe off and put the sock on over their own sock and stand up.

The first team with a sock-wearing house elf is the winner!

Patronus

&

Dementor

You'll need at least 6 people for this game, but the more the better.

Have all the players spread out in an open area, like a large room or a yard.

Now, all the players should silently choose one person to be their Patronus and one person to be their Dementor. They should keep this information to themselves.

Instruct the players to try to stay away from their Dementor, and at the same time, try to get behind their Patronus to protect themselves from their Dementor.

Let the players run for 3-5 minutes. Once they're thoroughly exhausted, stop everyone and have them guess who picked them as a Dementor and who picked them as a Patronus.

This game results in a lot of laughs and confusion when one player's Patronus is running in terror from them and one player can't move because three players have picked him as their Patronus.

Quidditch

Quidditch Supplies

1. You'll need to make two Quidditch hoops. To do this, you'll need two hula hoops and two long stakes that are 2-3 feet long. Take one hula hoop and, using packing tape or duct tape, tape it on top of one stake, so it looks like a giant lollipop. You're going to need a lot of tape to make it stable, so just keep taping!

    When you're done, spray paint it entirely brown. You now have a Quidditch hoop! Create the other Quidditch hoop, and then stake them into the ground on opposite ends of your yard.

2. Next, buy some hacky sacks or bean bags. These will be the bludgers. Make sure that whatever you buy or make is about the size of a tennis ball and is very soft. The Quidditch players will be throwing these at each other, and we don't want anyone to have to go see Madam Pomfrey.

3. You'll need a snitch. You can either buy a licensed plastic snitch or make one from a gold ball and a couple of feathers.

4. Lastly, you'll need a quaffle. You can take any kind of ball -- soccer ball, volleyball, kickball -- and spray paint it brown. Voila! A quaffle.

Object of the Game

• The object of the game is to get the quaffle through the opposing team's Quidditch hoop as many times as possible. The teams score 1 point per goal.

Here's the catch -- there will be bludgers lying all around the Quidditch field. At any time, any player can pick up a bludger and throw it at the player holding the ball. If the player holding the ball is hit, he must throw or drop the ball immediately.

• One player on each team will be a seeker. That means they'll spend the game looking for the snitch.

• The game ends when one of the seekers finds the snitch. The team whose seeker finds the snitch wins an extra 3 points.

• Hide the snitch well, making it difficult to find. When the game starts, the seekers must go look for the snitch.

• There should be an equal number of players on each team.

Tip: If you have a large yard, don't put out too many bludgers or players will never get a quaffle through the hoop. If you have a small yard, use more bludgers or players will be making it through the hoop every few seconds.

Silly

&

Riddikulous

This is a silly game that is geared toward younger kids, though a lot of older kids will get a kick out of it, too.

Make a dementor costume or buy one online or from a Halloween shop (try to get one on sale after Halloween ends), stuff it, and tie a string from the top of its head.

Next, put strips of black velcro all over the dementor -- the face, the legs, the arms, the stomach, the back... everywhere!

Now get out some accessories like feather boas, old coin purses, old costume jewelry, and put strips of velcro on the back side of them. If you don't have any feather boas and costume jewelry lying around, check your local thrift store. They're loaded with old lady supplies.

Hang your dementor from a tree and put all your accessories in a box near the dementor.

Instruct players to try to stick the accessories to the dementor after you shout "Riddikulous!" and begin swinging the dementor from the tree like a pinata.

When you shout "Riddikulous!" the second time, they must stop.

Players earn 1 point for each item they were able to stick to the dementor.

Hermione had trouble perfecting her Patronus charm because most of her happy memories are about getting good grades, and those aren't quite powerful enough to make a Patronus. What is her Patronus?

Answer: An Otter

The Gnome Throw

This is a simple game for younger kids.

Buy several Styrofoam balls and paint gnome faces on them. Beards are not optional. Paint blue hats on half of the gnomes and green hats on the other half.

Take several bins or buckets, tie a rope on them, and hang them from a tree. If you don't have a tree or don't like the idea of putting a bunch of buckets in it, you can just place them around your yard.

Throw the gnomes (balls) all over the yard and tell the players that you need their help removing the gnomes by throwing them into the buckets.

Split players into teams and have them only remove the gnomes of their team's colors.

Start some music or set a timer, and when the time is up, count the number of gnomes each team was able to remove.

Alternative Version: Have each player throw a gnome as far as he can. Mark the spot where the gnome fell when he threw it.

The player who throws the gnome the farthest wins!

Tri-Wizard

Tournament

For this game, you're going to need lots and lots of large boxes. Some good options for finding these for free are: appliance stores, furniture stores, and Craigslist.

Create a maze with your boxes by using them as walls and using duct tape to keep them together.

Keep the tops of your boxes intact so that the maze is dark inside.

Cut small holes in the boxes or string twinkle lights through it so that players can see where they're going when they're inside.

Up the scary factor by hanging rubber snakes and spiders from the tops of the boxes and putting gummy worms and bubble wrap on the floor.

Time each player with a stopwatch from the time they enter to the time they exit.

The fastest player to get out of the maze is the champion!

Werewolf Attack

Everybody knows that if you get bit by a werewolf you'll either become a werewolf yourself or get a nasty infection.

In this game, one player will start as the werewolf. The rest of the players hide from the werewolf. The werewolf will go stalking for the other players and if he finds one and tags him, that player becomes a werewolf, too. They then go stalking together.

The game ends when all the players have been turned into werewolves. At that point, you better get them into the Shrieking Shack before the neighbors see them.

CHAPTER III

TREATS

$\mathscr{N}$o party is complete without treats, especially a Harry Potter party! Go all out with the following recipes to let your guests celebrate Hogwarts style. From Acid Pops to Pygmy Puff Pastries, your guests will think they just stepped off the Hogwart's Express with their bellies filled with sweets.

Harry, Ron, and Hermione had their first great adventure during a troll attack in *Sorcerer's Stone*, so a platter full of Troll Eyes is fitting for this feast. Before returning to class, students might want to package up an Owl Snack to take to the Owlery. Hedwig and Pigwidgeon will be most appreciative.

Don't forget to use the great Potion recipes in this chapter to make all your other adventures turn out perfectly...or, should we say, "Prefectly"?

Saving the Wizarding world is hard work. Young witches and wizards are sure to love all the tasty treats and refreshing drinks featured in this chapter.

Acid Pops

INGREDIENTS

1/2 cup of Honey

Lollipops

Pop Rocks Candy

DIRECTIONS

I.   Remove lollipops from wrappers.

II.   Dip a lollipop into the honey.

III. Then dip it into the pop rocks until you've covered it completely.

Enjoy a popping, tingling surprise when you bite into your acid pops.

Chocolate Wands

Long Pretzel Sticks

Chocolate

I.   Melt chocolate by putting it into a pot and putting that pot over a pot of boiling water. This will melt the chocolate without burning it.

II. Dip the pretzel stick into the chocolate until you've covered it completely. Let dry.

III. Add texture, vines, or handles with a squeezable icing pouch.

Chocolate Frogs

Gummy Frogs

Chocolate

Instead of breaking your back over dozens of little frog molds, try this easier method.

I.   Melt chocolate by putting it into a pot and putting that pot over a pot of boiling water. This will melt the chocolate without burning it.

II.   Dip your gummy frogs in the chocolate and let them cool at room temperature.

Tast-easy chocolate frogs!

Toad Eggs in Jelly

INGREDIENTS

1 Package of Lime Jell-O

1 Passion Fruit

DIRECTIONS

I.   Cut open the passion fruit and scrape out all the slimy green seeds that look like toad eggs.

II.   Mix the passion fruit seeds with the lime Jell-O and boiling water (check the instructions on your Jell-O package for exact measurements) and refrigerate until solid. Yum!

Dragon Eggs

Cadbury Eggs

Silver Luster Dust

Edible Glitter

Vanilla Extract

I. Remove the Cadbury Eggs from their wrappings.

II. Put a few drops of vanilla extract in a cup.

III. Dip a small paint brush in the vanilla extract and then into the silver luster dust.

IV. Paint the luster dust onto the eggs.

V. Sprinkle edible glitter on the tops and sides of the eggs before the luster dust dries.

These are a sweet, sweet dragon egg treat.

Flobberworms

Brown Gummy Worms

Oreos

I. Crumble the oreos and pour them into a box or bowl labeled "Flobberworms."

II. Add the brown gummy worms.

If you can find it, the gummy lettuce in gummy burgers makes a great meal for the flobberworms.

Troll Eyes

INGREDIENTS

Frozen Meatballs

Mozzerella Cheese

Sliced Black Olives

DIRECTIONS

I. Follow the baking directions on the frozen meatball packaging.

II. Cut circles out of the mozzarella cheese using a small round cookie cutter.

III. Top each meatball with a round slice of cheese and a sliced black olive.

IV. Bake for an additional 2-3 minutes, or until the cheese has melted.

Owl Snack

INGREDIENTS

White Chocolate

Hershey's Kisses

Twizzlers

Almond Slices

Large Marshmallows

DIRECTIONS

I.   Cut a large marshmallow in half. This will serve as the mouse's body.

II.   Melt the white chocolate by putting it in a pot and setting that pot over a pot of boiling water. This will keep the chocolate from burning.

III.   Dip the marshmallow half into the white chocolate and then stick the chocolate kiss and almond slices on it to form the head.

IV.   Wait for the body to dry, then dip the head in the chocolate or drizzle the chocolate over the head.

V.   Use a toothpick to poke a hole into the back of the marshmallow.

VI.   Pull apart a Twizzler until you have a small strip of it and insert that strip into the back of the marshmallow for the tail.

Yum! Mice for dessert!

Pensieve Potion

INGREDIENTS

2 Liter Bottle of Sprite

Silver Edible Glitter

DIRECTIONS

I.   Fill 1/4 of a large punch bowl with water.

II.   Place a photo or illustration at the bottom of the bowl to serve as the "memory" that can be seen in the pensieve.

III. Put the bowl in the freezer until the water has turned to ice.

IV. Fill the rest of the bowl with Sprite and add a dusting of edible silver glitter to the top.

Polyjuice Potion

INGREDIENTS

2 Liter Bottle of Orange Soda

1 Bag of Gummy Body Parts

Gold Edible Glitter

DIRECTIONS

Combine all the ingredients in a large punch bowl and you've got one disgusting-looking potion on your hands. Kids will love it.

Tip: Add a strainer spoon to the bowl for those who would prefer not to choke on a gummy fingertip.

Luck Potion

Cream Soda

Gold Edible Glitter

I. Combine ingredients and fill tiny, corked glass bottles with it.
II. Label the bottles with parchment paper that reads, "Felix Felicis".

Lucky and delicious!

Pumpkin Juice

1/2 cup Canned Pumpkin

1 cup Vanilla Ice Cream

1 cup Milk

1/2 teaspoon Pumpkin Pie Spice

1/4 teaspoon Vanilla Extract

Combine all the ingredients in a blender and blend until smooth.

Makes 4 creamy and refreshing pumpkin juices.

Pygmy Puff Pastries

Pink Snowballs

Gumballs

Black Food Marker

I.   Remove the Snowballs from the packaging and mold them into a slightly rounder shape.

II.   Take your gumballs and draw black circles on them to look like eyes.

III.   Push the gumballs into the Snowballs so that the black circles are centered in the middle.

You are now the proud owner of some delicious pygmy puff pastries.

*W*e hope you have been inspired by the suggestions presented in this book. Use an assortment of these ideas together to create a perfectly wonderful party, or allow your imagination to come up with even more. The possibilities are endless.

Bring your favorite characters and memories to life by weaving scenes from the story into your party. Every Harry Potter fan—whether they have only seen a couple movies or are HP aficionados—will find themselves getting caught up in the excitement.

Your party can be as simple or complex as you want it to be. If time is limited, make crafts beforehand and select games with minimal preparation. Once the magic begins, there is no telling where it will end.

Remember, many of these suggestions also make great family fun ideas. The next time you settle in to watch your favorite Harry Potter movie, make up a batch of tasty Chocolate Wands to snack on. Yum!

Here's one last tip for making your party a complete success. If you need guests to leave the room while you set up a new game, send them outside to hunt for those pesky Nargles. Luna could really use some help getting her shoes back.

Your only job now, as Headmaster of this party, is to watch your guests have a Harry Potter party experience they'll never forget.

14431236R00068

Made in the USA
Charleston, SC
11 September 2012